IMAGES
of America
SAN FRANCISCO'S
CHINATOWN

THE CHINESE HISTORICAL SOCIETY OF AMERICA (CHSA). Founded in 1963, CHSA is dedicated to fostering an understanding of the Chinese American experience through exhibitions, education, research, and publications. Its Museum and Learning Center, located in the landmark Julia Morgan YWCA building at 965 Clay Street in San Francisco, features the main exhibition, "The Chinese of America: Toward a More Perfect Union," as well as rotating exhibits of visual artists and distinct aspects of Chinese Americana. CHSA publishes a monthly newsletter and an annual journal, *Chinese America: History and Perspectives*. For more information, visit http://www.chsa.org.

ON THE COVER: This publicity photograph of three boys building a sand pyramid at the corner of Grant Avenue and Pine Street was released by the San Francisco Chamber of Commerce sometime in the 1930s. (Courtesy of California Historical Society.)

IMAGES
of America

SAN FRANCISCO'S
CHINATOWN

Judy Yung and the
Chinese Historical Society of America

ARCADIA
PUBLISHING

Published by Arcadia Publishing
Charleston SC, Chicago IL, Portsmouth NH, San Francisco CA

Printed in the United States of America

Library of Congress Catalog Card Number: 2006921510

For all general information contact Arcadia Publishing at:
Telephone 843-853-2070
Fax 843-853-0044
E-mail sales@arcadiapublishing.com
For customer service and orders:
Toll-Free 1-888-313-2665

Visit us on the Internet at www.arcadiapublishing.com

This book is dedicated to my parents Tom Yip Jing and Jew Law Ying, who chose to make our home in San Francisco's Chinatown.

PORTSMOUTH SQUARE, 1946. Author Judy Yung was born in San Francisco's Chinatown, the youngest of five girls, from left to right, Sandra, Patricia, Judy, Sharon, and Virginia. A sixth child, Warren, was born two years later.

CONTENTS

ACKNOWLEDGMENTS

My deepest appreciation goes to Philip P. Choy, Sue Lee, and Ruthanne Lum McCunn for serving as advisors on this book project; William Wong and the editorial staff at Arcadia Publishing for sharing their expertise; Elaine Joe for graphic design; Ben Chan, Frank Jang, and Paul Lam for volunteering their photography services; and the Seligman Foundation for their generous funding.

Without the assistance and generosity of the following people, this book of photographs would not have been possible: Ted Fang, *Asian Week*; Susan Snyder and Therese Salazar, Bancroft Library, University of California, Berkeley; Joe Evans, California Historical Society; Doreen Der-McLeod, Cameron House; Cathie Lam, Chinatown Community Development Center; Elaine Tom, Chinese Recreational Center; Wei Chi Poon, Ethnic Studies Library, University of California, Berkeley; Cynthia Westbrook Hu, San Francisco Convention and Visitors Bureau; Susan Goldstein, San Francisco Public Library; Gianna Capecci, Society of California Pioneers; Robert Chandler, Wells Fargo Bank; Kari Lee, Chinatown YMCA; Philip P. Choy; Chris Huie; Calvin Jew; Steve Louie; Felicia Lowe; Russell Lowe; Ruthanne Lum McCunn; Douglas Wong; Henry Woon; and Connie Young Yu.

I wish to also thank John Chan, Joyce Chan, Gordon Chin, Calvin Fung, Edward Fung, Fair Fung, Him Mark Lai, Benjamin Lee, Sandra Lee, Deborah Murphy, and Gavin Ng for their research assistance and support.

ABOUT THE AUTHOR

Judy Yung is professor emerita of American Studies at the University of California, Santa Cruz. Dr. Yung is currently working on her husband's memoirs, *The Adventures of Eddie Fung: Chinatown Kid, Texas Cowboy, and POW Survivor*.

She has worked as a librarian at the Chinatown Branch Library in San Francisco and the Asian Branch Library in Oakland, as associate editor of *East/West* newspaper, and director of the Chinese Women of America Research Project in San Francisco. Her books include *Island: Poetry and History of Chinese Immigrants on Angel Island, 1910–1940* (1980); *Unbound Feet: A Social History of Chinese Women in San Francisco* (1995); *Unbound Voices: A Documentary History of Chinese Women in San Francisco* (1999); and *Chinese American Voices: From the Gold Rush to the Present* (2006).

INTRODUCTION

San Francisco's Chinatown has the reputation for being the oldest, largest, and most famous Chinese enclave outside of Asia. Bordering Nob Hill on the west, the financial district on the east, and North Beach on the north, Chinatown dates back to the 1850s, when 30,000 Chinese from Guangdong Province came for the California gold rush. Some settled in the vicinity of Portsmouth Square, establishing businesses to serve the growing population in San Francisco. After the gold rush was over, many more Chinese men, recruited to build the railroads and work in agriculture and manufacturing, came. By 1882, when Congress passed the Chinese Exclusion Act, prohibiting the further immigration of Chinese laborers to this country, Chinatown had grown to 15,000 people, occupying the 12-block area that remains its core today.

Early Chinese settlers called Chinatown Tong Yun Fow or "town of the Tang people," so named because of their reverence for the Tang Dynasty. On the one hand, they chose to live in this neighborhood because it provided them with everything they needed—work, food and supplies, mutual aid organizations, religious houses, medical care, entertainment, and newspapers. On the other hand, racial discrimination and hostilities in the 1870s prevented them from finding better jobs and housing outside Chinatown and from sending for their wives in China. It wasn't long before Chinatown turned into an overcrowded slum, notorious for its tong wars, opium dens, and prostitution. Tourists came to Chinatown as much to see this underworld as to shop for exotic curios from the "Orient."

When all of Chinatown was destroyed in the 1906 earthquake and fire and the city made plans to move Chinatown to a less desirable location, Chinese merchants acted quickly to rebuild on the original location. The new "Oriental City," designed in a "faux-Chinese" style to attract tourists, was cleaner, safer, and more modern. Moreover, the earthquake, in destroying all the birth certificates in city hall, provided a way for Chinese immigrants to circumvent the unjust exclusion laws by claiming U.S. citizenship and sending for their families in China. Slowly Chinatown's population grew from a low of 8,000 in 1920 to 18,000 by the eve of World War II. The streets of Chinatown bustled with shoppers, tourists, and family life. Prevented from integrating into the larger society, however, Chinese remained stuck in Chinatown, living in crowded quarters and working menial jobs.

It was not until World War II, when China and the United States became allies that conditions improved for Chinese Americans. Congress repealed the Chinese Exclusion Act, granting Chinese the right to become naturalized citizens and allowing a small number of Chinese immigrants to come to this country. In the following decades, many anti-Chinese laws were revoked, enabling Chinese to marry whites, own land, find better jobs, and live outside Chinatown. People began moving to other parts of the city and to the suburbs, leaving behind the elderly, single men, and low-income families. If not for the booming tourist trade and increased immigration in response to the War Brides Act and, more importantly, the Immigration Act of 1965, Chinatown would have become a ghost town.

As a result of renewed immigration, the Chinese population in San Francisco grew from 25,000 in 1950 to 82,000 in 1980. The influx of Chinese immigrants and families revitalized Chinatown, providing it with a large labor force while creating new demands for Chinese food, goods, and services. The streets of Chinatown teemed with life again. Tourism remained Chinatown's top moneymaker, but behind the glitz, ghetto conditions of substandard housing, low-wage jobs, inadequate health care, and street crime began taking their toll. In response, a new generation of Chinese American activists, inspired by the civil rights movement, organized demonstrations, lobbied all levels of government for funding, and established over 30 new organizations to deal with the community's many socioeconomic problems. Then in 1989, San Francisco was hit by the Loma Prieta earthquake, which seriously damaged the Embarcadero Freeway, Chinatown's primary vehicular artery. When the city decided to demolish the freeway despite the pleas of the community, Chinatown suffered such severe economic hardship that its future vitality became uncertain.

Recovery has been slow. Chinatown now ranks as the third rather than second most visited attraction in San Francisco, after Fisherman's Wharf and Union Square. But throughout its history, Chinatown has never been just a tourist attraction. To this day, it exists simultaneously as a residential neighborhood, business community, and cultural center for Chinese Americans of diverse backgrounds. The images collected in this book document the realities of daily life and major transformations in the past 150 years. They also attest to the tenacity and skills of a community to overcome adversity and maintain Chinatown as a vibrant place for residents, businesses, and tourists.

One

TONG YUN FOW

1848–1906

PORTSMOUTH PLAZA, C. 1865. Chinatown was born in the vicinity of Portsmouth Plaza, which was barren land just 20 years before this photograph was taken. Known as the "Cradle of San Francisco," it was here that navy captain John B. Montgomery planted the American flag on July 9, 1846, claiming the Mexican port of Yerba Buena for the United States; here that newspaper editor Samuel Brannan sparked the gold rush by running through the plaza yelling, "Gold on the American River;" and here that Mayor Geary and a committee of San Franciscans officially welcomed 300 "China Boys," presenting them with Christian literature in Chinese on August 28, 1850. (Courtesy of Society of California Pioneers.)

PARROTT BUILDING, C. 1876. Chinese labor was instrumental in the building of San Francisco. The John Parrott Building at the corner of California and Montgomery Streets was built in 1852 by Chinese masons using granite stone cut to specification from China. The construction was so sturdy that the building withstood the 1906 earthquake. (Courtesy of CHSA collection.)

CHINESE CIGAR FACTORY ON MERCHANT STREET, 1869. As mining declined in the late 1850s, manufacturing became San Francisco's chief economic base. Chinese workers, generally paid less than white workers, were hired to make cigars, shoes, clothing, and woolens. Many Chinese opened their own factories in Chinatown after they learned the trade. (Courtesy of Bancroft Library, University of California, Berkeley.)

CHINESE FISHERMEN, C. 1897. As early as 1854, about 150 Chinese fishermen settled on the south side of Rincon Point, operating 25 boats and catching 3,000 pounds of fish a day. These two fishermen are drying shrimp and squid to be sold locally or shipped to China, Japan, and the Hawaiian Islands. (Courtesy of CHSA collection.)

CHINESE VEGETABLE GARDEN, C. 1885. Initially Chinese could live and work anywhere. Some grew vegetables for the local market. The Chinese in this photograph are tending a vegetable garden at Union and Pierce Streets—then the outskirts of the city. (Courtesy of California Historical Society.)

WING CHUN LAUNDRY AT 2460 SACRAMENTO STREET, 1906. With the shortage of female labor and a willingness on the part of the Chinese to take on any gainful job, many Chinese operated laundries or worked as cooks and domestics outside Chinatown. (Courtesy of Philip P. Choy.)

TONG YUN GAI, 1865. Sacramento Street, between Stockton and Kearny Streets, became known as Tong Yun Gai (street of the people of the Tang Dynasty) because it was here that the first Chinese stores and organizations were established in the early 1850s. (Courtesy of Society of California Pioneers.)

DUPONT STREET, C. 1880. As the original inhabitants vacated buildings along Dupont Street (later renamed Grant Avenue) and moved to other parts of the city, Chinese became the new tenants. They operated storefronts at the street level and shared boarding rooms behind and above the stores. To further maximize space use, they sometimes added balconies and awnings to the front of the buildings. (Photograph by Isaiah West Taber; courtesy of Bancroft Library, University of California, Berkeley.)

DUPONT AND CLAY STREETS, 1900. By the 1870s, Dupont Street had replaced Sacramento Street as the economic center of Chinatown. A directory published by the Wells Fargo Bank in 1878 listed 423 Chinese firms, with 121 located on Dupont Street, 60 on Sacramento Street, and 60 on Jackson Street. (Courtesy of Bancroft Library, University of California, Berkeley.)

CLAY STREET ABOVE DUPONT, C. 1900. Chinese had a distinctive way of decorating the old Italianate Victorian buildings. They placed flowerpots on the balconies, hung big red lanterns from the canopies, and affixed Chinese signboards to the walls. The Chinese sign on the left is an advertisement for a restaurant: "Will arrange banquets—full line of light refreshments available." (Courtesy of CHSA collection.)

HANG FAR LOW RESTAURANT, 1885. Among the earliest banquet-size Chinese restaurants in San Francisco, Hang Far Low operated continuously at 713 Dupont Street until it was sold in 1960 and renamed Four Seas Restaurant. (Courtesy of Bancroft Library, University of California, Berkeley.)

THE GRAND DINING ROOM, C. 1882. The top floor of Hang Far Low Restaurant—replete with inlaid panels, carved screens, and hardwood tables and stools imported from China—was reserved for the Chinese elite and their guests. (Photograph by Isaiah West Taber; courtesy of Bancroft Library, University of California, Berkeley.)

COMMON DINING ROOM, C. 1911. The middle floor of Hang Far Low housed the kitchen and served more common fare to Chinese shopkeepers and workers during the day. Some restaurants offered monthly coupons for meals at different prices. Cheaper restaurants that served simple rice and noodle dishes were usually located in the basements of buildings. (Photograph by Louis J. Stellman; courtesy of Society of California Pioneers.)

CHINESE PHARMACY. When sick, people would go to an herbalist for a pulse diagnosis and prescription. A prescription usually contained 10 to 15 varieties of herbs, barks, roots, nuts, and flowers—all imported from China and stored in unmarked drawers behind the store's counter. (Courtesy of Wells Fargo Bank.)

CHY LUNG BAZAAR, 1866. Among the early Chinese settlers were merchants like Lai Chu-chuen. Upon arrival in 1850, he opened Chinatown's first bazaar at 640 Sacramento Street, importing teas, opium, silk, lacquered goods, and Chinese groceries. Although he passed away in 1869, the Chy Lung store remained in business until 1912. (Courtesy of Wells Fargo Bank.)

INTERIOR OF A CHINESE STORE, C. 1904. A typical dry goods store had shelves and cabinets to the ceiling filled with merchandise. At the back of the store was an altar table. The chairs lined on the side were used for entertaining guests and customers. (Courtesy of Bancroft Library, University of California, Berkeley.)

CORNER OF DUPONT AND CLAY STREETS, 1900. The Tie Yick general store was known for their preserved meats—dried duck, pig livers, oysters, and frogs. Note the cable car tracks on the cobblestone street and the men reading handwritten notices and ads on the brick wall. (Photograph by Laura Adams Armer; courtesy of California Historical Society.)

BUTCHER AND GROCERY STORE, C. 1880. Storefronts were often opened to the street so that meat and produce could be displayed on hooks, racks, and counters along the sidewalk. (Photograph by Isaiah West Taber; courtesy of Bancroft Library, University of California, Berkeley.)

STREET PEDDLER, C. 1900. Since there was no refrigeration, people had to purchase fresh food daily. Here a woman inspects a live chicken in a peddler's basket on Washington Street below Dupont Street. (Photograph by Arnold Genthe; courtesy of CHSA collection.)

WOOD CHOPPERS, C. 1900. Wood choppers serviced homes with wood-burning stoves. Here they are entering Ross Alley off Washington Street. Above the men hangs the sign of a pawnshop, strategically located near the gambling rooms in the area. (Courtesy of San Francisco Public Library.)

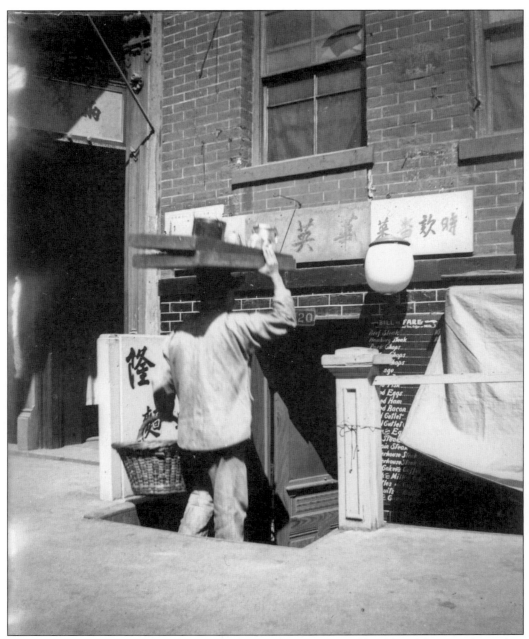

CHINESE WAITER, 1900. Until the 1940s, Chinatown restaurants offered free deliveries of complete meals to the home, and it was a common sight to see waiters in the street balancing a wooden tray full of covered dishes on their heads. This waiter is returning to a Chinese restaurant that serves Western food. Note the "Bill of Fare" on the right advertising beefsteak for 10¢. (Photograph by D. H. Wulzen; courtesy of San Francisco Public Library.)

STREET COBBLER, 1900. The streets of Chinatown were filled with itinerant peddlers and artisans—tinsmiths, umbrella repairmen, pipe bowl cleaners, jewelers, and cobblers—all plying their trades. (Photograph by Charles Weidner; courtesy of California Historical Society.)

FORTUNE TELLER, C. 1900. For a small fee, the fortune teller would help those who were illiterate write letters home. It was customary for Chinese immigrants to periodically send remittances, accompanied by a letter, to their families in China. (Courtesy of CHSA collection.)

23

WASHINGTON PLACE, 1880. Alleys were important commercial frontages and a reminder of similar passageways in the villages of Guangdong Province. The Tuck Hing meat market, located at the left corner of the alley, operated for 100 years (from 1888 to 1988) in the same location. (Photograph by Isaiah West Taber; courtesy California State Library.)

FISH ALLEY, C. 1906. The Chinese had their own names for the alleys in Chinatown. They referred to Washington Place (later renamed Wentworth Alley) as Fish Alley because of the many shops there that specialized in processing and selling fish. (Courtesy Library of Congress.)

TIEN HOU TEMPLE, C. 1910.
The Chinese called Waverly
Place Tien Hou Miu Gai after the
temple built in honor of Tien Hou,
Goddess of Heaven and protector
of travelers, writers, actors, sailors,
and prostitutes. Erected in 1852
under the auspices of the Sam Yup
District Association, the temple was
destroyed in the 1906 earthquake
and rebuilt on the top floor of the
Shew Hing District Association
building at 125 Waverly Place.
(Courtesy of CHSA collection.)

BARBER SHOP, 1879. Waverly Place was
also known as Ho Boon Gai (Fifteen Cent
Street) because the Chinese barbershops
on the street charged 15¢ for a haircut.
Until the Qing Dynasty was overthrown
in 1911, all Chinese males were required
to comb their hair in a long braid or
queue as a sign of loyalty to the Manchu
emperor. The 15¢ haircut included
shaving the forehead, brushing and
braiding the queue, and cleaning the ears.
(Courtesy of Philip P. Choy.)

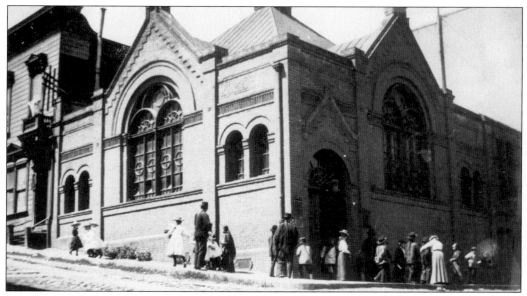

FIRST CHINESE BAPTIST CHURCH, C. 1906. Churches of various denominations provided English classes for adults, Sunday school for children, and social services for the needy. Located at the corner of Waverly Place and Sacramento Street, the First Chinese Baptist Church was established in 1887 and rebuilt with the same clinker bricks after it was destroyed in the 1906 earthquake. (Courtesy of Bancroft Library, University of California, Berkeley.)

KONG CHOW TEMPLE AT 512 PINE STREET, C. 1869. The majority of Chinese immigrants practiced an eclectic mix of ancestral worship, Taoism, and Buddhism. The Kong Chow Temple, built by the Sun Wui District Association in honor of Guan Gung, God of War and Literature, had a Victorian arch cornice crowning the top of the facade and a marble slab with gilt Chinese characters bearing the temple's name. The temple was moved to the top floor of the U.S. Post Office at Clay Street and Stockton Street in 1977. (Courtesy of Philip P. Choy.)

CHEE KUNG TONG AT 36 SPOFFORD ALLEY, 1907. This fraternal organization, also known as the Chinese Free Masons, has existed in Chinatown since the 1850s. A branch of the Triad Society in China, it advocated the overthrow of the Qing Dynasty and the restoration of the Ming emperor to the throne. The Tong later functioned as a major support center for Dr. Sun Yat-sen's successful 1911 revolution in China. (Courtesy of San Francisco Public Library.)

INTERIOR OF THE DONN QUAI THEATER, c. 1880. Cantonese opera followed Chinese immigrants to America. In 1852, the Hong Fook Tong from China performed the first opera in San Francisco. By the 1870s, there were at least four theaters in Chinatown. Donn Quai Yuen on Jackson Street had the seating capacity for several hundred people. Merchants and their families sat in the choice box seats, women in the curtained lodges, and workers on wooden benches on the main floor. The stage was bare except for the musicians, who sat in the center on stools behind the actors. The Chinese banner above the stage reads, "When ideals are in harmony, the sounds that ensue will be elegant." (Courtesy of Bancroft Library, University of California, Berkeley.)

ENTRY OF THE GENERAL, 1883. Attending the opera was a noisy, festive, and drawn-out affair, as the audience smoked, ate, and chatted throughout the performance, which sometimes lasted all day. Audiences were generally familiar with the plots and arias of the popular historical plays and famous classics. Here a general makes his grand entrance in a performance at the Donn Quai Theater. (Photograph by Isaiah West Taber; based on a painting by Theodore Wores; courtesy of California State Library.)

OPIUM ROOM, C. 1890. Popularly advertised as laudanum in the Sears Roebuck catalog and not outlawed until 1909, opium was used by Chinese immigrants as a means of relaxation and escape from the drudgery of daily life. Opium rooms, such as this one, were clustered around Duncombe Alley and Jackson Street. (Courtesy of Library of Congress.)

CHINESE BROTHEL, C. 1890. Prostitution was rampant in 19th-century San Francisco, including the predominantly male society of Chinatown, where brothels, such as this one, lined Bartlett and Sullivan Alleys. Unlike white prostitutes who plied their trade as free agents at the south end of Chinatown, most Chinese prostitutes had been sold by poor parents in China and brought to America to work as indentured slave girls. (Photograph by Theo Marceau; courtesy of Bancroft Library, University of California, Berkeley.)

METHODIST MISSION HOME, C. 1880. Some slave girls escaped enslavement by being redeemed, running away with a lover, or seeking refuge at a mission home. The Chinese Methodist Episcopal Mission at 940 Washington Street was established by Rev. Otis Gibson in 1870 to educate and convert the Chinese to Christianity, as well as to provide shelter for Chinese prostitutes and homeless girls. Rebuilt after the 1906 earthquake, it now serves as the Gum Moon Women's Residence. (Courtesy of Philip P. Choy.)

PRESBYTERIAN MISSION HOME, C. 1915. Many Chinese slave girls found refuge at the Presbyterian Mission Home, whose superintendents, Margaret Culbertson and Donaldina Cameron (back center), raided brothels with the help of the police. Located at the corner of Sacramento Street and Joice Alley, the mission was renamed Donaldina Cameron House in 1942 and continues to serve Chinatown today by providing assistance to youth, women, and families in need. (Photograph by Louis J. Stellman; courtesy of California State Library.)

CHINATOWN SQUAD, 1898. In the overcrowded male society of Chinatown, social vices and criminal activities sometimes got out of hand. The police department attempted to curb such activities by establishing the Chinatown Squad in 1875. Pictured here with their interpreter Dong Gong and the tools of their trade, the squad was known for its zealousness in combating gambling, prostitution, and tong violence. (Courtesy of CHSA collection.)

COURTYARD BEHIND JACKSON STREET, 1890s. The population in Chinatown grew to 20,000, all packed into a 12-block area. This courtyard served as a common kitchen for the three tenement buildings surrounding it. The poor living conditions were mostly caused by the negligence of white slumlords and the discriminatory housing practices that prevented Chinese from owning property or living outside Chinatown. (Photograph by Arnold Genthe; courtesy of CHSA collection.)

OUTDOOR KITCHEN, C. 1900. Because of the cramped living conditions and lack of indoor plumbing, residents often had to do their washing and cooking in common kitchens or outdoors. (Courtesy of CHSA collection.)

MERCHANT CLASS, 1898. Merchants, who were exempted from the 1882 Chinese Exclusion Act, were allowed to bring their families to America. Pictured here are Lew Kan, a labor contractor and owner of the Fook On Lung store on Sacramento Street, and his two sons. (Photograph by Arnold Genthe; courtesy of CHSA collection.)

GOLDEN GATE PARK, 1890s. Occasionally a merchant would rent a horse and buggy and take his family to Golden Gate Park or the Cliff House. Because Chinese customs at that time decreed that proper women should not be seen in public, this was a rare sight. (Courtesy of Bancroft Library, University of California, Berkeley.)

THE SUE FAMILY IN CHINATOWN, 1904. By becoming a partner in a local business, some laborers were able to claim merchant status and send for their wives in China. However, even wives of laborers, like Mrs. Sue in this photograph, seldom appeared in public. According to her oldest child Alice (middle), Mrs. Sue rarely left the house except to attend the Chinese opera or New Year festivities. (Photograph by Arnold Genthe; courtesy of Library of Congress.)

CHINATOWN BOYS, C. 1898.
Children were precious in the
tight-knit community of bachelors.
Here two Chinese boys are enticing
passersby to place bets on their
sidewalk lottery board. (Photograph
by Floyd Lumbard; courtesy of
Connie Young Yu.)

**PUPILS OF THE METHODIST MISSION
HOME, C. 1906.** Chinese girls were
not held in the same esteem as boys.
As Chinese prostitution declined
at the end of the 19th century, the
staff at the Methodist Mission Home
began turning their attention to
providing a home and education for
abandoned Chinese girls.
Note these girls, unlike most
Chinatown children, are dressed
in Western clothing. (Courtesy
of Bancroft Library, University of
California, Berkeley.)

MISS CABLE'S CLASS, 1882. The Occidental School was started by Rev. William Speer in the basement of the Presbyterian Chinese Mission on Stockton Street in 1853. When the school began receiving public funds in 1859, it became the first public school in the United States for Chinese students. Note that both boys and girls are in this class. (Photograph by Isaiah West Taber; courtesy of Bancroft Library, University of California, Berkeley.)

CHINESE PRIMARY SCHOOL. In 1887, after the courts ruled in *Tape v. Hurley* that the San Francisco Board of Education had to admit Chinese children into the public schools, the city established another facility for Chinese children at 920 Clay Street. The Chinese Primary School was renamed Oriental Public School in 1906 to accommodate Japanese and Korean children. (Courtesy of California Historical Society.)

CHINESE CLUB ROOM, 1890s. As Chinatown grew, the power of merchants expanded to brokering jobs and dominating district and clan associations. Common geographical origins or surnames were the basis for membership in these associations, which arbitrated disputes and provided its members with shelter, food, medical care, social activities, and funeral services. (Courtesy of Bancroft Library, University of California, Berkeley.)

OFFICERS OF THE CHINESE SIX COMPANIES, 1890s. Six district associations banded together in the 1860s as the Chinese Six Companies to settle disputes between district associations, fight anti-Chinese laws, and speak on behalf of the Chinese community. They were formally established as the Chinese Consolidated Benevolent Association in 1882. (Courtesy of Bancroft Library, University of California, Berkeley.)

FUNERAL PROCESSION ON DUPONT STREET, C. 1915. Prominent Chinese who passed away were accorded elaborate funerals, which included family members dressed in sackcloth, Taoist and Buddhist priests, a horse-drawn hearse, and a marching band—in this case the Cathay Boys Band. After a period of time, the bones were exhumed and shipped to China for reburial. (Courtesy of CHSA collection.)

DEDICATION OF THE TUNG WAH DISPENSARY, 1900. The Chinese Six Companies succeeded in leading an effort to establish a small clinic on Sacramento Street that provided care for the sick and terminally ill. The clinic offered both Chinese and Western medicine. (Courtesy of CHSA collection.)

NARCISSUS FLOWER VENDOR, 1890s. During Chinese New Year celebrations, streets were filled with vendors and people shopping for the traditional fruits and flowers that symbolize good luck and prosperity. (Photograph by Arnold Genthe; courtesy of CHSA collection.)

CHINESE NEW YEAR PARADE, 1885. The golden dragon dance ends the New Year parade and 15-day celebration in Chinatown. A beneficent creature of strength and goodness, the block-long dragon is usually preceded by a round red object representing the pearl of potentiality. (Courtesy of Bancroft Library, University of California, Berkeley.)

THE EARTHQUAKE AND FIRE FROM CLAY STREET. According to Chinese beliefs, the Earth Dragon stirred at 5:12 a.m. on April 18, 1906, and caused a massive earthquake that lasted 47 seconds. This was followed by three days of raging fire, inextinguishable because of the broken water mains. Chinatown was reduced to rubble and ashes after the first night. (Photograph by Arnold Genthe; courtesy of Library of Congress.)

REFUGEES FROM CHINATOWN, 1906. The earthquake and fire left more than half of the city's residents and all of Chinatown's homeless. Pausing at Bush and Battery Streets, these Chinese refugees prepare to leave their homes for temporary shelter at Golden Gate Park, the Presidio, Oakland, and other parts of the Bay Area. (Photograph by Laura Adams Armer; courtesy of California Historical Society.)

Two

ORIENTAL CITY
1906–1945

Chinatown, San Francisco, California.

GRANT AVENUE LOOKING NORTH, C. 1910. Within six days after the earthquake and fire, the city made secret plans to move Chinatown to the mud flats in Hunter's Point. But stiff resistance from the Chinese government, the fear of losing tax revenues and China trade, and quick action on the part of leading Chinese merchants led to the rebuilding of Chinatown in its original location. (Courtesy of Philip P. Choy.)

SING CHONG BAZAAR, 1910. American-born entrepreneur Look Tin Eli took the lead in creating the pseudo-Chinese facade that would become Chinatown's distinctive trademark. He hired the architect and engineer team of Ross and Bungren to build the Sing Chong bazaar at the northwest corner of Grant Avenue and California Street, instructing them to make it look "emphatically Oriental." They did this by placing a pagoda tower on top of the four-story building and decorating the exterior with Chinese motifs and colors. The large bay windows on the upper floors were for displaying Oriental furniture, which the store carried, along with curios, silks, and art goods from China and Japan. (Courtesy of California Historical Society.)

Sing Fat Bazaar, 1915. Merchant Tong Bong followed Look Tin Eli's lead and had Ross and Bungren design the Sing Fat bazaar across the street from Sing Chong in a similar fashion, with a pagoda tower perched on top and dragon trademarks below the tower. The two corner buildings dominated the skyline at the south end of Grant Avenue, serving as gateways to the new Oriental City. (Courtesy of Bancroft Library, University of California, Berkeley.)

CHINATOWN TELEPHONE EXCHANGE, 1909. Chinatown's telephone exchange was rebuilt in the style of a three-tiered pagoda but had to be squeezed between two buildings because of its narrow lot at 743 Washington Street. Starting with 800 subscribers, the exchange served Chinatown under manual operation until 1949, when the system was converted to dial phones. The building was then sold to the Bank of Canton. (Courtesy of Bancroft Library, University of California, Berkeley.)

INTERIOR SWITCHBOARD, 1935. The Chinese-styled interior—black lacquered walls trimmed in red and gold and an ebony-finished switchboard with two golden dragons above—was both functional and decorative. In 1935, the Chinatown Telephone Exchange employed 21 female operators who, together, handled an average of 13,000 calls per day. (Courtesy of CHSA collection.)

LEE FAMILY ASSOCIATION BUILDING. Family and district associations that had the financial resources were among the first to rebuild after the 1906 earthquake. The Lee Family Association moved into this brick building at 916 Grant Avenue in 1919. Typical of the new association buildings that made up the core of Chinatown, it was designed for mixed use—commercial space on the ground floor, apartments in the middle, and the association headquarters on the prestigious top floor. (Photograph by Brian W. Choy.)

MAN FUNG WO, 1908. In the rebuilding process, many of the Chinese groceries and merchandising stores became concentrated on the 700 to 900 blocks of Grant Avenue, between Sacramento and Jackson Streets. Here two workers are moving sacks of rice outside Man Fung Wo, a butcher and grocery store located at 921 Grant Avenue. (Courtesy of Bancroft Library, University of California, Berkeley.)

INTERIOR OF SANG WO, 1908. This meat and grocery store, located at 867 Grant Avenue from 1868 to 1978, was a popular place to shop. Alice Sue, who grew up in Chinatown in the early 1900s, remembers shopping there for pork, tofu, bean sprouts, and "whatever vegetables my mother wanted." (Courtesy of San Francisco Public Library.)

SHOPPING FOR PRODUCE, 1900S. Storefronts shifted from common open fronts to glass window commercial frontages. As before, however, produce and goods spilled over into the sidewalks. (Courtesy of Bancroft Library, University of California, Berkeley.)

CHINESE NEWSBOY, 1910. At the time that this photograph was taken, there were four Chinese dailies published in San Francisco: *Chung Sai Yat Po* (Chinese-American daily), *Sai Gai Yat Po* (Chinese World), *Tai Tung Yat Po* (China Free Press), and *Young China*—all espousing different political views on the future of China. (Courtesy of CHSA collection.)

PORTOLA PARADE, 1909. All of Chinatown took part in the Portola Festival to celebrate the rebirth of the city. As seen in this photograph, the woman warrior Fa Mulan—resplendent in red silk armor and headdress—acted as the parade marshal. (Photograph by Louis J. Stellman; courtesy of California State Library.)

DOUBLE TEN PARADE, 1912. Thanks to the financial support of overseas Chinese communities, Dr. Sun Yat-sen's Revolutionary Party succeeded in overthrowing the Qing Dynasty on October 10, 1911, and establishing the Republic of China. A parade to celebrate the birth of the new republic was held in San Francisco and, in subsequent years, every October 10. (Photograph by Louis J. Stellman; courtesy of California State Library.)

SPOFFORD ALLEY LOOKING SOUTH, C. 1915. Commonly known as "Sun Louie Sung Hong" or "New Spanish Alley" to the Chinese because of the many Spaniards who used to visit the gambling houses and brothels there, Spofford Alley was also known as a stronghold of Dr. Sun Yat-sen's revolutionary cause. Note the flags of the new Republic of China and the tall door gods on the left guarding the building from evil spirits. (Photograph by Louis J. Stellman; courtesy of CHSA collection.)

WOMAN WITH BOUND FEET, 1908. The new republic encouraged men to cut their queues and women to unbind their feet. Here a servant holds a child while another servant assists the mistress with bound feet—a sign of beauty and gentility in old China. (Photograph by Louis J. Stellman; Courtesy of CHSA collection.)

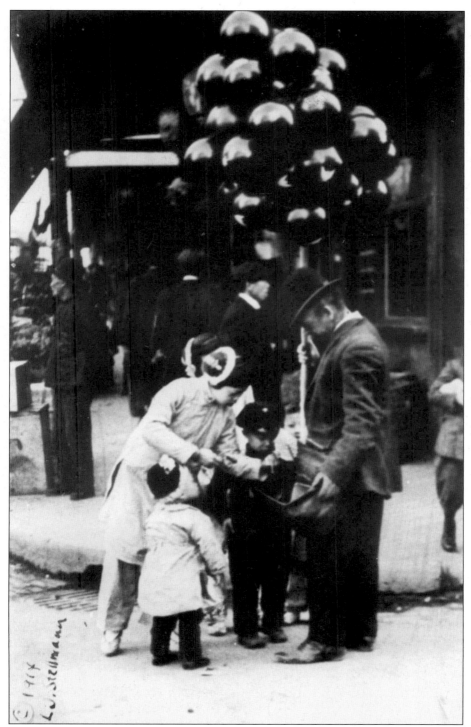

THE BALLOON MAN, 1914. The rebuilding of Chinatown after the 1906 earthquake, combined with the founding of the new republic, ushered Chinatown into the modern era. The old-fashioned balloon man remained a fixture on Grant Avenue, but note the children's Western dress and the newly paved sidewalk. (Photograph by Louis J. Stellman; courtesy of CHSA collection.)

NEW YEAR BLOSSOMS, 1914. Chinatown prepares for another New Year celebration on Grant Avenue but without queues and traditional Chinese clothing. (Photograph by Louis J. Stellman; courtesy of CHSA collection.)

SIDEWALK VENDOR, C. 1915. The new Chinatown featured sidewalk stands, such as this one, offering fruit, snacks, cigarettes, and sundries. At closing time, the vendor would tuck away all protruding merchandise, slide boards into grooves in the stand, and padlock the end of each groove. (Photograph by Mervyn Silberstein; courtesy of California Historical Society.)

STOCKTON STREET LOOKING NORTH, 1925. After the core of Chinatown was rebuilt along and around Grant Avenue, other areas began to fill in, up to and along Stockton Street, where a concentration of religious institutions and commercial structures developed. The Chinese Six Companies is on the left side of the street behind the iron gate, St. Mary's Chinese School sits on the northeast corner of Stockton and Clay Streets, and two other churches—the Presbyterian Church in Chinatown and the Chinese United Methodist Church—are located on the east side of Stockton Street. (Courtesy of Bancroft Library, University of California, Berkeley.)

INTERIOR OF THE CHINESE SIX COMPANIES HEADQUARTERS. Chinese merchants, now dressed in Western suits, continued to dominate the Chinese Six Companies and to rule Chinatown. (Courtesy of CHSA collection.)

CHINESE AMERICAN CITIZENS ALLIANCE (CACA) CONVENTION, 1923. Originally established as the Native Sons of the Golden State (NSGS) to combat anti-Chinese sentiment and advance the concerns of the American-born generation, the organization changed its name to CACA in 1915 to accommodate lodges outside of California. Its national headquarters at 1044 Stockton Street was completed in 1921. (Photograph by Harry Jew; courtesy of CHSA collection.)

PEACE MEETING BETWEEN HIP SING TONG AND BING KUNG TONG, 1921. Internecine feuds among certain tongs over control of underworld activities, such as gambling and prostitution, had been escalating since the late 1880s. The establishment of the Peace Society in 1913 helped to resolve some of the disputes. Still, in 1921, Inspector John Manion (left) of the Chinatown Squad was called upon to help mediate a truce between the two leading tongs. (Courtesy of Bancroft Library, University of California, Berkeley.)

PUBLIC BURNING OF OPIUM ON WASHINGTON STREET, 1914. In an effort to maintain law and order, as well as improve Chinatown's image, community leaders worked with federal officials to crack down on illegal drug use. (Courtesy of Society of California Pioneers.)

A Family at the Corner of Grant Avenue and Clay Street, 1927. As the population of first generation males declined due to the effects of the Chinese Exclusion Act, the relative proportion of families and children increased. After the earthquake destroyed all the birth records in city hall, some Chinese immigrants were able to claim U.S. citizenship and thereby send for their wives and children in China. By 1920, the Chinese male to female ratio had declined from 27 to 1 in 1890 to 4 to 1; and the proportion of native-born Americans had increased from 2.7 to 30 percent of the Chinese population in the United States. (Photograph by Arnold Genthe; courtesy of Bancroft Library, University of California, Berkeley.)

WAITER, 1920s. Chinese immigrants lacking English proficiency and education had limited job opportunities. Most of the men did menial labor in Chinatown restaurants, stores, and laundries. (Courtesy of CHSA collection.)

GARMENT WORKER, 1936. Most of the women—more than 1,000 of them—worked in 69 garment factories in Chinatown, toiling under sweatshop conditions: poor lighting and ventilation, long hours, and low piece-rate wages. (Courtesy of San Francisco Public Library.)

LILY YIP PICKETING NATIONAL DOLLAR STORES, 1938. Over 100 garment workers at the Chinese-owned National Dollar Stores factory made Chinatown history when they went on strike for 13 weeks and won an agreement for higher wages and improved benefits. (Courtesy of *Chinese Digest.*)

A Crowded Kitchen in Chinatown, 1940. Since few apartments were built after the earthquake and housing discrimination prevented Chinese from living outside Chinatown, many families had to live in cramped residential hotels intended for singe men. It was common for a family of six or eight to occupy two rooms and share a toilet and kitchen with neighbors on the same floor. (Courtesy of San Francisco Public Library.)

Bathhouse on Stockton Street, 1952. Bathhouses provided segregated bathing facilities for men and women who did not have private bathrooms at home. (Courtesy of San Francisco Public Library.)

DRYING FISH, 1922. Chinatown residents and businesses made use of all available space, including drying laundry and fish on the rooftops. (Courtesy of CHSA collection.)

CHINESE YMCA SWIMMING POOL, 1936. The YMCA provided Chinatown with its only swimming pool. Here 11-year-old Norman Ong demonstrates his jack-the-knife dive at the YMCA's 25th anniversary swimming exhibition. (Courtesy of Chinatown YMCA.)

CHINESE YMCA, 1927. Many modern organizations were established in the community in the 1920s to meet the social and educational needs of the younger generation. The Chinese YMCA first opened a facility on Stockton Street in 1911 to introduce boys to American-style sports, music, and technical skills. A more spacious building at 855 Sacramento Street was completed in 1926 that included a swimming pool, gym, dormitory rooms, and meeting space for classes and club activities. (Courtesy of Chinatown YMCA.)

CHINESE YWCA ACTIVITIES, 1920S. First established in 1916 at an abandoned saloon on Sacramento Street, the YWCA provided educational classes, recreational activities, bathing facilities, and social services for girls and young women in Chinatown. In 1932, members raised enough money for a new building at 965 Clay Street that was designed by Julia Morgan (see page 2). (Courtesy of CHSA collection.)

CHINESE PLAYGROUND, 1948. This half-acre playground, built in 1927 on Sacramento Street between Hang Ah Alley and Waverly Place, was, for many years, the only play area for children and teens in all of Chinatown. In this photograph, the volleyball and tennis courts are on the top level facing Hang Ah Alley, and the clubhouse and children's play area are on the middle level. Not visible is a basketball court on the bottom level facing Waverly Place. The playground was renovated in the 1980s and, in 2006, it was renamed Willie Woo Woo Wong Playground after a prominent Chinese American basketball player. (Courtesy of San Francisco Public Library.)

OPPOSITE: CHINATOWN LIBRARY, 1921. Given the crowded living conditions in Chinatown, the North Beach Branch of the San Francisco Public Library was a popular place for children to study and borrow books to read. Located at 1135 Powell Street, this Carnegie building was renamed the Chinatown Branch when a branch in the North Beach district opened in 1958. The interior of the Chinatown Branch was completely retrofitted and renovated in 1996. (Courtesy of San Francisco Public Library.)

NAM KUE CHINESE SCHOOL AT 755 SACRAMENTO STREET. In the mid-1930s, there were 10 Chinese schools in Chinatown with a total attendance of 2,000 students. The Nam Kue School, built in 1925 for the children of immigrants from Namhoi District, features traditional Chinese architectural motifs—tile roofs, glazed terra cotta animal figures, window lattices, and lanterns—but does not resemble any known prototype in China. (Courtesy of California Historical Society.)

CALLIGRAPHY CLASS, 1944. Children generally attended Chinese school from 5:00 p.m. to 8:00 p.m. on weekdays and often on Saturday mornings. The curriculum covered Chinese classics, history and geography, calligraphy, composition, ethics, and use of the abacus. Tuition ranged from $2 to $5 per month. (Photograph by James Wong Howe; courtesy of Bancroft Library, University of California, Berkeley.)

DOUBLE TEN PARADE, 1942. Many of the Chinese schools had drum and bugle corps or marching units that participated in Chinatown parades and festivals. These two photographs show boys and girls from Hip Wo Chinese School marching in the parade to celebrate the founding of the Chinese republic. Housed in the Chinese United Methodist Church at Washington and Stockton Streets, the Hip Wo School was established in 1925 through the combined efforts of four Chinatown churches. (Photographs by Harry Jew; courtesy of CHSA collection.)

CHINESE NURSERY SCHOOL, 1934. Thanks in part to President Roosevelt's New Deal during the Great Depression, Chinatown was able to open a much-needed nursery school at the Chinese YWCA. The Chinese Presbyterian church provided yard space on Joice Street for the 33 children who were enrolled in the program. (Courtesy of San Francisco Public Library.)

ARCHITECTS OF THE ORIENT, 1930s. This publicity photograph of three boys building a sand pyramid at the corner of Grant Avenue and Pine Street was released by the San Francisco Chamber of Commerce with a caption that reflects the attitude of the period: "A real sand man left this pile of sand in San Francisco's picturesque Chinatown, never dreaming that it would be used by Chinese kiddies to re-create the temples of their celestial ancestors." (Courtesy of California Historical Society.)

SUNDAY AFTERNOON AT THE SHEE WONG CHAN'S, 1944. This photograph of Grandpa Chan reading the Sunday paper with his two grandsons was part of a larger group of photographs commissioned by *Look* magazine to document the assimilation of Chinese Americans and their allegiance to the U.S. cause in World War II. (Photograph by James Wong Howe; courtesy of Bancroft Library, University of California, Berkeley.)

INTERIOR OF A PAWNSHOP, 1944. This unusual photograph reveals the setup in most Chinatown pawnshops, where the customer remained hidden from view because it was considered disgraceful to pawn anything. According to the photograph caption in *Look* magazine, "Shops do less business than normal because of war prosperity." Yick Lung, the last pawnshop in Chinatown, closed in 1969. (Photograph by James Wong Howe; courtesy of Bancroft Library, University of California, Berkeley.)

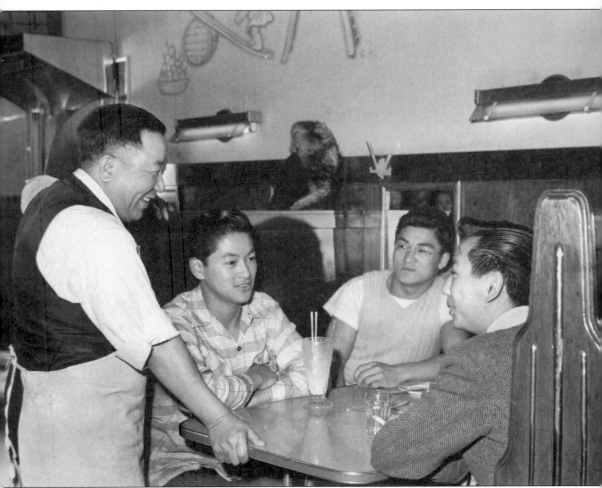

FONG FONG, 1944. In 1935, George Kao (left) opened Chinatown's first modern bakery and soda fountain on Grant Avenue, with an ice cream maker capable of producing 50 gallons per hour and an automatic donut machine that turned out 20 dozen donuts per hour. Fong Fong was known for such unique flavors as ginger and lichee ice cream and the chop suey sundae, which consisted of Chinese fruit cream, crushed fruit toppings, whipped cream, and sesame cookies. The business closed in 1975. (Photograph by James Wong Howe; courtesy of Bancroft Library, University of California, Berkeley.)

GRANDVIEW THEATER AT 756 JACKSON STREET, 1940S. Chinese movies replaced Chinese opera as the most popular form of entertainment in the 1930s. In 1940, filmmaker Joseph Sunn Joe opened Grandview Theater—Chinatown's first modern movie theater, complete with a neon-banded marquee, plush carpets, and uniformed usherettes. A dime admission purchased a newsreel, cartoons in English, and a main attraction in Cantonese. (Courtesy of National Archives.)

GOLDEN STAR RADIO, 1940S. From 1939 to 1979, the Golden Star Chinese Hour provided Chinatown with the latest news and entertainment on KBRG-FM (105.3 FM). Every weeknight from 9:00 p.m. to 11:00 p.m. and every Saturday from 3:00 p.m. to 5:00 p.m., families and businesses tuned in to hear Mary Chinn Tong (right) deliver the news on events in China, the United States, and the Chinese American community from her husband, Thomas Tong's, studio at 846 Clay Street. (Courtesy of National Archives.)

THE CATHAYAN ORCHESTRA AT THE ST. FRANCIS HOTEL, 1953. Second-generation Chinese Americans, drawn to the music of the Big Band era, organized their own dance bands and brought the popular music of America "live" into the community. Every weekend, the YWCA gym or the CACA hall was jammed with second-generation Chinese Americans, dancing the fox trot to the music of the Cathayans or the Chinatown Knights, another popular band at this time. (Courtesy of CHSA collection.)

FORBIDDEN CITY NIGHTCLUB, 1954. Nightclubs featuring dancing and floor shows sprang up in the late 1930s to capitalize on the growing numbers of affluent Americanized Chinese and white tourists. Started by entrepreneur Charlie Low in 1938, Forbidden City was located at 363 Sutter Street, a block from the "entrance" to Chinatown at Bush Street and Grant Avenue. A popular nightspot, it attracted movie stars, public figures, soldiers on leave, and even heads of state. (Courtesy of the documentary, *Forbidden City, U.S.A.*, directed by Arthur Dong, DeepFocus Productions.)

FORBIDDEN CITY FLOOR SHOW, 1940s. Like the Cotton Club in Harlem, which featured America's finest black entertainers, Forbidden City gained an international reputation with its unique showcase of Chinese American performers. Its one-hour show, performed three times every evening, consisted of musical and dance acts, slapstick, tap dancing, magic acts, and chorus lines. (Courtesy of the documentary, *Forbidden City, U.S.A.*, directed by Arthur Dong, DeepFocus Productions.)

RICE BOWL PARTY, 1938. After Japan attacked China in 1937, Chinese Americans rallied behind the war effort in China. San Francisco's Chinatown hosted the first of three Rice Bowl parties in 1938. More than 200,000 people packed the confetti-filled streets and alleys to enjoy the parade, fashion shows, cultural performances, and street carnival. Through such fund-raising efforts, Chinatown was able to send $5 million—the largest amount from any Chinese American community—to China. (Courtesy of *Chinese Digest*.)

RICE BOWL PARADE, 1940. It took at least 50 to 100 women to carry the Chinese flag in the Rice Bowl parade. Bystanders would throw money into the flag to be sent to China for war relief. (Photograph by Harry Jew; courtesy of CHSA collection.)

CLOSEOUT SALES ON GRANT AVENUE, 1942. Japanese-owned stores, concentrated at the south end of Grant Avenue, had to clear out within a few days after Japanese Americans, following Japan's attack on Pearl Harbor, were ordered to evacuate the West Coast and were interred in desolate areas of the country. Few returned to Grant Avenue after the war. (Photograph by Bill Koska; courtesy of San Francisco Public Library.)

SELLING WAR BONDS, 1942. Chinatown emptied its pockets for the U.S. war chest in World War II. The Chinese chapter of the American Women's Volunteer Services sold $1,000 worth of war bonds each day at their booth on Grant Avenue. (Courtesy of Martha Taam.)

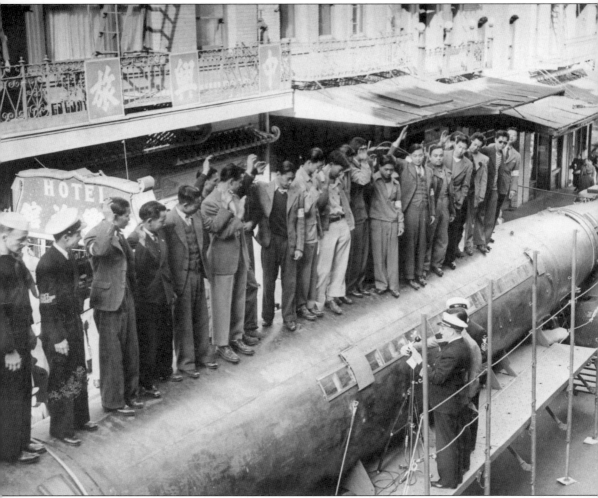

NAVY DAY CEREMONIES ON GRANT AVENUE, 1942. Many Chinese Americans, out of a strong sense of Chinese nationalism and American patriotism, enlisted in the U.S. armed forces in World War II. Here a group of Chinese American recruits for the U.S. Navy take their oath on top of a captured Japanese submarine on tour in San Francisco. (Courtesy of San Francisco Public Library.)

MADAME CHIANG AT THE CHINESE SIX COMPANIES, 1943. As part of her nationwide tour to drum up U.S. support for the war in China, Madame Chiang Kai-shek stopped by San Francisco for a six-day visit. (Photograph by Kem Lee.)

CHINATOWN PARADE, 1943. Elaborate parades and receptions in Chinatown, as well as in the Civic Center, were held in Madame Chiang's honor during her visit. (Photograph by Douglas Wong.)

VICTORY PARADE, 1945. Lai Yee Guey, a seamstress and mother of six children, proudly marches in the V-J Day parade in Chinatown to celebrate the end of World War II. (Courtesy of Lorena How.)

Three

GILDED GHETTO
1945–2000

GRANT AVENUE LOOKING SOUTH, 1944. "Largest Chinatown outside of China—a kaleidoscope of Oriental fascinations," read the caption for this magazine ad. Behind the gilded facade, however, was a ghetto beset with growing pains and political conflicts. (Courtesy of Felicia Lowe.)

AERIAL VIEW OF BRENHAM PLACE FROM KEARNY STREET, 1945. Portsmouth Square trees are in the foreground, Clay Street is on the left side, and Nob Hill is west above Chinatown. At the time this photograph was taken, 17,000 adults and 6,000 children lived in a 20-block area, constituting the highest density and tuberculosis rate of any neighborhood in San Francisco. (Courtesy of San Francisco Public Library.)

CHONG JAN COMPANY AT 930 GRANT AVENUE, 1947. Newly renovated businesses along Grant Avenue were a sign of the booming postwar economy and an improvement in the socioeconomic status of Chinese Americans. (Courtesy of San Francisco Public Library.)

KUO WAH CAFÉ AT 950 GRANT AVENUE, 1947. Another sign of the prosperous times, Kuo Wah Café was actually five enterprises under one roof: a main restaurant, famous for its dim sum, roast beef, and chicken chow mein; a soda fountain, featuring hot apple pie and sesame soup; the Lion's Den, a cocktail bar and nightclub; a bakery in the basement; and a residential hotel on the upper floors. (Courtesy of San Francisco Public Library.)

TOURISM ON THE RISE. According to Ching Wah Lee, art dealer and tour guide, the number of paying tourists in Chinatown shot up from 50,000 to 75,000 annually after the war. In this photograph taken in 1947, Jane Lau shows visiting Rotarians from North Carolina how to use chopsticks. (Courtesy of San Francisco Public Library.)

Memorial Day at St. Mary's Square, 1951. Over 2,000 people attend the dedication ceremonies for a memorial plaque to honor 90 Chinese Americans from San Francisco who died in World War I and II. In the background is a statue of Dr. Sun Yat-sen, father of the Chinese republic, sculpted by Benjamino Bufano. (Photograph by Kem Lee; courtesy of Connie Young Yu.)

English Class at the Chinese YWCA, 1948. Close to 6,000 Chinese women immigrated to the United States after Congress passed the War Brides and Chinese Alien Wives Acts. Many settled in urban Chinatowns, where they could find cultural sustenance, jobs, and assistance in adjusting to American life. As a result, the Chinese male to female ratio narrowed to two to one in 1950. (Courtesy of San Francisco Public Library.)

STUDENTS PLEDGING ALLEGIANCE TO THE FLAG, 1946. Commodore Stockton Elementary School (formerly Oriental Public School) had the highest enrollment of students in the city. The school remained all Chinese until desegregation through busing was enforced in the 1970s. In 1998, the school was renamed Gordon J. Lau after the first Chinese American to be elected to the board of supervisors. (Courtesy of San Francisco Public Library.)

INTERSECTION OF WASHINGTON AND STOCKTON STREET, 1947. Pedestrian traffic at this intersection was heavy after 3:00 p.m. on school days, when students were release from Commodore Stockton and were on their way to Hip Wo Chinese School. (Courtesy of San Francisco Public Library.)

AFTER SCHOOL SNACKS, 1949. Sherman Fong, who grew up in the 1940s, remembers Mrs. Lee's store at Stockton and Clay Streets, which sold slush cups, frozen bananas and cantaloupes, crispy noodles, and her famous curry potato-noodles served in a cardboard container. (Photograph by Benjamen Chin.)

CONCESSION STAND, 1949. Sherman Fong also remembers buying comic books, beef jerky, wax bottles filled with punch, roasted chicken gizzards, and cooked pine nuts at corner concession stands. (Photograph by Benjamen Chin.)

SPOFFORD ALLEY LOOKING NORTH, 1951. As housing discrimination lessened and Chinese were allowed to own land, people began to leave Chinatown for other parts of the city—North Beach, Russian Hill, Richmond, and Sunset districts. Those left behind were the elderly, single males, and low-income families. (See page 51 for an earlier photograph of Spofford Alley.) (Courtesy of San Francisco Public Library.)

DEDICATION OF THE PING YUEN HOUSING PROJECT, 1951. After 12 years of the community clamoring for low-cost public housing, three six-story buildings called the Ping Yuen (Tranquil Gardens) projects were finally built on Pacific Avenue between Columbus Avenue and Stockton Street. A fourth building, consisting of 12 stories with 150 units for families and 44 units for the elderly, was completed on the north side of Pacific Avenue in 1961. (Courtesy of San Francisco Public Library.)

INTERIOR OF ONE OF THE APARTMENT UNITS, 1951. Among 600 applicants for 234 apartments, one lucky family enjoys the comforts of their new home. (Courtesy of San Francisco Public Library.)

OCTOBER FIRST CELEBRATION, 1949. After Mao Tse-Tung's Communist Party defeated Chiang Kai-shek's Kuomingtang (KMT) to establish the Peoples' Republic of China, supporters of the new China celebrated at the Chinese American Citizens Alliance hall. Soon after this photograph was taken, tong men hired by KMT supporters stormed the hall and disrupted the meeting. The anti-Communist hysteria of the cold war era succeeded in driving the political left underground. The banners on stage read, "Arise, all overseas Chinese, and help build a new China. Long live the goodwill between Chinese and American people. (Courtesy of CHSA collection.)

BRENHAM PLACE (NOW WALTER U. LUM PLACE), 1958. As shown by the posters on the wall, Chinese Americans were also participating in American politics. (Courtesy of San Francisco Public Library.)

JULY FOURTH BEAUTY CONTEST, 1951. First sponsored by CACA in 1948, the bathing suit beauty contest here shows the degree to which second-generation Chinese Americans were adopting mainstream values and practices. (Courtesy of CHSA collection.)

CHINESE FOLK DANCE ASSOCIATION, 1960s. Chinese Americans also embraced Chinese traditional culture. Founded in 1959 by Jackson Chan (center), this group promoted Chinese culture through dance, choral, orchestral music, and martial arts. Still active today, the association specializes in folk dances from China's minority regions. (Courtesy of Steve Louie.)

LITTER BASKETS ON GRANT AVENUE, 1961. Col. John Young and Bernard Croty, members of the Chinatown Litter Control Committee, install litter baskets and bilingual signs along Grant Avenue. The signs were paid for by the Chinese Chamber of Commerce, an organization founded in 1908 to represent the interest of small businesses in Chinatown. (Courtesy of San Francisco Public Library.)

TOURISM ALONG GRANT AVENUE, 1960s. By now, tourism had become San Francisco's top industry and Chinatown's economic mainstay. Tourist traffic was particularly heavy at the south end of Grant Avenue, where curio stores selling trinkets, toys, art goods, housewares, and souvenirs were concentrated. (Photographs by Harry Jew; courtesy of CHSA collection.)

GRANT AVENUE BETWEEN PACIFIC AND BROADWAY, 1969. Markets, stores, and restaurants at the north end of Grant Avenue from Clay Street to Broadway Street catered to the everyday needs of the growing immigrant population. (Photograph by Harry Jew; courtesy of CHSA collection.)

NEWSSTAND AT THE SUN SING THEATER, 1021 GRANT AVENUE, 1969. This reader is catching up with the news offered by one of five daily newspapers published in Chinatown at this time. (Photograph by Harry Jew, courtesy of CHSA collection.)

ITALIAN MARKET AT GRANT AND JACKSON, 1969. Now closed, the Italian Market was a popular store for poultry and deli food. (Photograph by Harry Jew, Courtesy of CHSA collection.)

STREET CARNIVAL AT PORTSMOUTH SQUARE, 1969. Beginning in 1953, the Chinese Chamber of Commerce, in an effort to promote business and draw tourists to Chinatown, transformed the Chinese New Year celebration from a private family affair into a commercial venture. Portsmouth Square was turned into a street carnival with rides for children and concession games for prizes. (Photograph by Harry Jew; courtesy of CHSA collection.)

MISS CHINATOWN BEAUTY CONTEST, 1969. To draw even more public attention to the New Year festivities, the Chinese Chamber of Commerce launched the first Miss Chinatown, U.S.A. beauty pageant in 1958. Emulating the Miss America pageant, the criteria used to pick the winners were beauty, personality, and talent. (Photograph by Harry Jew; courtesy of CHSA collection.)

PARADE AUDIENCE AT THE CHINATOWN GATEWAY ON BUSH STREET, 1976. Each year, the grand parade became bigger and more commercial. Now marching units and floats from outside the community outnumber local units, and tourists outnumber local Chinese in the audience. (Courtesy of San Francisco Visitors and Convention Bureau.)

GUM LUNG, 1969. To this day, the Golden Dragon continues to end the Chinese New Year parade. (Photograph by Harry Jew; courtesy of CHSA collection.)

CHINATOWN'S FIRST DEMONSTRATION, 1968. Adopting the tactics of the civil rights movement, 200 demonstrators marched through Chinatown to a rally at Portsmouth Square. They criticized the Chinatown establishment for promoting tourism instead of resolving social problems in the community, and they called for reforms in the areas of education, employment, health, housing, youth, senior citizens, and immigration. (Photographs by Harry Jew; courtesy of CHSA collection.)

EDITORIAL
Violence in the streets

We hate to be alarmists, but someone has to point out the ominous trend that is taking shape in Chinatown today—violence in the streets.

One has but to glance at the lead story on the front page to note that within a span of a week, a number of assaults have taken place. Violence breeds violence. It could only end tragically. Next time there won't be just a bashed head, a bloody nose or a few missing teeth. Someone would be lying stone dead.

The time is now if we are to prevent the tragedy. The signs are there that it will happen if we do not shift course.

How? Wake up the community. This is not a nightmare that will vanish at dawn. It is a sickness, a wound that must be cauterized before gangrene sets in. This is a community problem that seeks and demands community action.

Violence in the streets is something new that confronts Chinatown. Heretofore, the Chinese are passive, meek, humble. Now there is a new breed, tough and arrogant. No one pushes them around. They are young animals, eager to hurt and be hurt.

We do not pretend to be any "ologist" that deals with abnormal and criminal behaviors. We do realize that these are young people under pressure to belong, to conform, and they are not making it and take it out on others. BULLSHIT!

We do not expect a miracle with just an editorial, but we do have hope that we might impress a few in the community who care, care about other people, care about the common problems we all face.

It is easy for us to write words. But we will work with anyone or any group if it concerns the welfare of Chinatown.

As for violence in the streets, that too can be overcome if enough people in our community take the initiative to do something about it.

BULLETIN BOARD AT LEWAY'S POOL HALL, 1968. Images of Chinese Americans as model minorities and Chinatown as a safe and quaint place to visit were shattered by rising juvenile delinquency and street crime. Organizations such as Leway (Legitimate Ways) formed to help high-school dropouts and foreign-born youths who were having trouble finding work and a place to belong. Their pool hall, located at 615 Jackson Street, served as a social and information center for over 300 Chinese youths a week. In 1977, the prophecy in the *East/West* editorial above came true when rivalry between two Chinatown youth gangs erupted in a shooting spree at the Golden Dragon Restaurant, leaving five people dead and 11 wounded. (Courtesy of *San Francisco Chronicle*.)

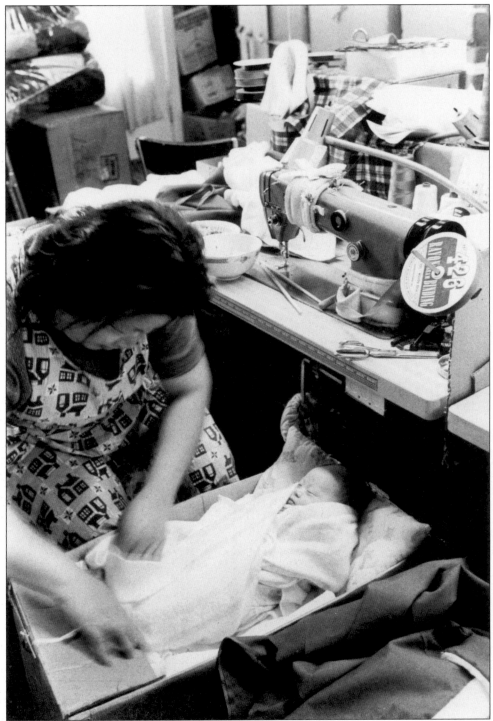

CHINATOWN GARMENT WORKER, 1977. As new immigrants flooded Chinatown's job market, wages and working conditions in the garment shops and restaurants deteriorated, despite efforts on the part of labor organizers and community activists to change the situation. (Photograph by Peter Man.)

CIVIC CENTER PROTEST, 1973. More than 500 Chinese parents, children, and community workers protest federal cutbacks in childcare funding. Only 10 percent of Chinatown's toddlers were receiving any childcare services at this time. (Photograph by Connie Hwang.)

WU YEE FIELD TRIP, 1999. As a result of these demonstrations, Wu Yee's Children's Services was established in 1977 to provide nutritious meals and educational activities for infants and toddlers from low-income families. Today Wu Yee operates six childcare centers in Chinatown, the Tenderloin, and Visitation Valley, with a total enrollment of 247 children of diverse ethnic backgrounds. (Courtesy of Wu Yee Children's Services.)

CHINESE SENIORS AT CITY HALL, 1972. Under the leadership of the Chinatown Coalition for Better Housing, three busloads of senior citizens descended upon the board of supervisors to show their support for low-cost senior housing in Chinatown. (Photograph by Byron Huey; courtesy of Cameron House.)

SELF-HELP FOR THE ELDERLY, 1979. President Johnson's War on Poverty program gave birth to new social service organizations staffed by bilingual community workers. Founded in 1966, Self-Help for the Elderly continues to provide job training, hot meals, social services, and housing assistance to seniors in Chinatown. (Photograph by Nancy Wang.)

MEI LUN YUEN HOUSING PROJECT. After 12 years of picketing, protesting, letter writing, and attending public hearings, the community finally got 185 units of housing for low-income families and the elderly built at the corner of Sacramento and Stockton Street in 1982. There were 3,500 applicants for the apartment units. Mei Lun Yuen (Garden of Beautiful Neighbors) is currently under the management of the Presbyterian Church in Chinatown. (Photograph by Paul Lam.)

INTERNATIONAL HOTEL AT KEARNY AND JACKSON STREETS, 1976. Built in 1907, the I-Hotel was home to some 160 Filipino and Chinese old-timers when it was sold to a private developer who wanted to build a multilevel parking garage. Tenants, with the help of Asian American activists, were able to delay eviction for nearly 10 years by filing lawsuits. Then in the early hours of August 4, 1977, 300 police officers in riot gear broke down the human chain of 5,000 protestors that had gathered around the hotel and dragged the remaining tenants out of the building. (Photograph by Chris Huie.)

New I-Hotel, 2005. The I-Hotel was demolished in 1979, but remained a hole in the ground for 17 years because of community demands that developers include low-cost senior housing in their plans. Finally in 1994, the Roman Catholic Archdiocese purchased the property for the new St. Mary's Chinese School, and the local community secured sufficient funds to build the new I-Hotel—a 15-story building with 104 units of affordable senior housing, a rooftop garden, and a Filipino American Cultural Center on the ground floor. (Photograph by Allen Liu; courtesy of Chinatown Community Development Center.)

CHINESE HOSPITAL ON JACKSON STREET. The original Chinese Hospital on the left was built in 1925 to replace the Tung Wah Dispensary on Sacramento Street (see page 39). Fifty years later, the hospital was deemed unsafe and out of date. The community raised the money to build the new 54-bed hospital beside it. The old building continues to be used for medical offices. (Photograph by Paul Lam.)

HANG AH ALLEY, 1980s. This alley, which faces Chinese Playground, is one of 41 historic alleyways being renovated by the Chinatown Community Development Center. The bottom photograph shows the alley after renovations in 1998. Founded in 1977, the Chinatown Community Development Center has done much to improve housing, parks and recreation, streets and alleyways, and transportation in Chinatown. (Courtesy of Chinatown Community Development Center.)

PORTSMOUTH SQUARE. Thanks to the efforts of the Park and Recreation Department, Portsmouth Plaza Parking Corporation, and Chinatown Community Development Center, major improvements to Portsmouth Square since the 1960s have included an underground garage, elevators and bathrooms, landscaping, safer play structures for the children, and an indoor recreation facility for seniors. (Photograph by Ben Chan.)

CIRCUS CLOWN AT PORTSMOUTH SQUARE, 1987. Schoolchildren enjoy a clown's antics when the circus came to Chinatown. (Photograph by Ben Chan.)

NORMALIZATION CELEBRATION, 1979. Hundreds gather in Portsmouth Square on New Year's Day to celebrate U.S. recognition of the People's Republic of China as the legitimate government of China and the normalization of relations between the two countries after a breach of 30 years. Although the historic event signaled the decline of KMT control over Chinatown, it did not end political conflicts over the two-China question. An equally large crowd of Taiwanese students from Bay Area colleges and universities held a rally at Washington Square in the North Beach District to protest U.S. recognition of Beijing. (Photograph by Steve Louie.)

CIVIC CENTER RALLY, 1989. After armed troops suppressed a student demonstration at Tienanmen Square, an estimated 100,000 people rallied to demand democratic reforms in China. Again Chinatown was divided over the issue. It took five years before an agreement could be reached to place a bronze replica of the Goddess of Democracy statue in Portsmouth Square. (Photograph by Ben Chan.)

VOTER REGISTRATION, 1977. Representing a new generation of political activists, Germaine Wong and Lillian Sing, volunteers with the Chinese American Voters Education Committee, encourage people in Chinatown to become registered voters. Wong would later become the city's registrar of voters and Sing, a municipal court judge. (Photograph by Gary Tom.)

M AND J CHILDREN'S STORE, 1977. Beginning in the late 1970s, many family businesses were forced to close because of higher rent bids from Hong Kong investors and new businesses catering to the tourist trade. Mable and Kew Yuen Ja, managers of M and J at 952 Grant Avenue for over 25 years, lost their lease when a curio shop offered the landlord triple their rent plus $20,000 "key money." (Courtesy of Chinatown Community Development Center.)

TIN BOW TONG, 1978. Similarly one of Chinatown's oldest herb stores at 947 Grant Avenue had to close when its landlord, Yan Wo Benevolent Association, accepted a higher rent bid from another shopkeeper. (Photograph by Harry Jew; courtesy of CHSA collection.)

SUN SING THEATER AT 1021 GRANT AVENUE, 1980s. As new immigrants turned to Chinese television, videotapes, and laserdiscs for their entertainment, Chinese opera and movie houses closed one after another. (Courtesy of Chinatown Community Development Center.)

SUN SING CENTER. Two of Chinatown's six movie houses—Grandview Theater on Jackson Street and Sun Sing Theater on Grant Avenue—were gutted and, respectively, turned into a Buddhist store and a shopping mall that sells clothing, housewares, electronics, and souvenirs. (Photograph by Paul Lam.)

VIETNAMESE RESTAURANT ON PACIFIC AVENUE. Many Vietnamese Chinese refugees settled in the vicinity of Chinatown after the Vietnam War ended. They, along with recent immigrants from Hong Kong and China, have replaced many of the old shopkeepers in Chinatown. (Courtesy of Chinatown Community Development Center.)

JEWELRY STORES IN THE 1980s. A study of Chinatown businesses in 1984 found a proliferation of banks and jewelry stores on Grant Avenue and Stockton Street. The banks tap into the saving habits of Chinese immigrants while the jewelry stores cater to both tourists and Chinese immigrants. A moratorium on new banks in Chinatown was passed by the city, and rezoning in 1986 had made it more difficult for tourist and gift shops to be established on Stockton Street. (Photograph by Harry Jew; courtesy of CHSA collection.)

STOCKTON STREET LOOKING NORTH. High rents on Grant Avenue have driven many neighborhood stores to Stockton Street, which is now the main shopping area for fresh produce, deli food, and groceries. (Photograph by Paul Lam.)

PRODUCE MARKET ON STOCKTON STREET. Following marketing practices in Asia, the new produce and grocery stores have open fronts and products on display out on the sidewalk, similar to Chinatown storefronts in the 1880s (see page 20). (Courtesy of Chinatown Community Development Center.)

LOWER GRANT AVENUE. Many Chinese curio shops and restaurants at the south end of Grant Avenue have been forced out of business by high rents due to the area's proximity to Union Square. Replacing them are stores with neon signs peddling discount cameras, luggage, T-shirts, and electronics that are out of character with Chinatown. (Photograph by Paul Lam.)

CHINATOWN SHUTDOWN TO PROTEST FREEWAY PLAN, 1990. Chinatown suffered little physical damage when the Loma Prieta earthquake hit in 1989. However, in the aftermath of the earthquake, tourism and business declined by 20 to 40 percent. Business people were alarmed when they heard that city hall, under pressure from environmentalists, planned to demolish the damaged freeway that was the primary vehicular entry to Chinatown. For the first time in Chinatown's history, almost all the businesses closed for three hours so that people could go protest the freeway plan. (Photograph by Eric Luse; courtesy of *San Francisco Chronicle*.)

OVERFLOW CROWD AT CITY HALL, 1990. Despite the large turnout and arguments from the community that closing down the freeway would hurt business in the Chinatown, North Beach, and Fishermen's Wharf areas, the board of supervisors voted to demolish rather than repair the freeway. As predicted, Chinatown businesses suffered huge losses when tourists and suburban Chinese found it inconvenient to get to Chinatown. (Photograph by Brant Ward; courtesy of *San Francisco Chronicle*.)

MOON FESTIVAL FAIR, 1995. Using city funds allocated to help merchants recover from the effects of the earthquake, the Chinatown Merchants Association responded to the economic slump by sponsoring the first annual Autumn Moon Festival on Grant Avenue—a one-day affair of live entertainment, food, arts and crafts, and a parade. (Photograph by Henry Woon; courtesy of Ethnic Studies Library, University of California, Berkeley.)

CHINATOWN NIGHT MARKET, 1999. Likewise, in an effort to revive Chinatown's nightlife, the Chinatown Neighborhood Association launched the first annual Night Market Fair at Portsmouth Square. Held on Saturday nights from May to November, the fair features cultural entertainment and booths selling souvenirs, arts and crafts, and bargain knickknacks. (Photograph by Gordon Mar; courtesy of Pius Lee.)

Four

CHINATOWN TODAY

CHINATOWN GATEWAY AT GRANT AVENUE AND BUSH STREET. Chinatown today is a complex overlay of multiple sites. It is a cultural link for Chinese Americans in the Bay Area, a gateway for recent immigrants, a regional tourist attraction, a shopping district, a place for small businesses to prosper, and home to more than 15,000 people—most of whom are foreign-born and elderly. The Chinese writing under the gateway comes from Dr. Sun Yat-sen's teachings: "When the Great Way prevails, all under Heaven will work for the people. First comes loyalty, filial devotion, kindness, and love; then faithfulness, justice, harmony, and peace." (Photograph by Paul Lam.)

LIFE IN CHINATOWN. Qiong Zhen Xu holds the trap with the 39th mouse that she has caught in her one-room apartment in six months. Despite the crowded living conditions, Qiong prefers to stay in Chinatown, where she can get around on her own, rather than move in with her daughter's family in the suburbs. (Photograph by Liz Hafalia; courtesy of *San Francisco Chronicle*.)

PING YUEN MURAL ON STOCKTON STREET. Painted by Darryl Mar in 1999, this mural depicts the colorful faces of real people in the community, their contributions and aspirations, as well as their remembrance of the past. (Photograph by Paul Lam.)

120

St. Mary's Square on November 12. Every year on the birthday of Dr. Sun Yat-sen, Chinatown elders gather at his statue to pay respect to the founding father of the Chinese republic. (Photograph by Ben Chan.)

Green Street Brass Band at Jackson Street and Grant Avenue. The tradition of the funeral procession continues today, but the remains of the deceased are no longer shipped back to China for reburial. (Photograph by Paul Lam.)

SAM WO RESTAURANT ON WASHINGTON STREET. First established in 1907, the narrowest restaurant in Chinatown is now taken over by tourists, but it still holds the reputation for having the best *jook* (rice gruel) in town. (Photograph by Paul Lam.)

CAMERON HOUSE CARNIVAL. Hundreds of Chinese Americans who once participated in Cameron House's youth clubs come back each May for the Cameron House carnival, a tradition started in 1950 to raise funds for its summer program. (Courtesy of Cameron House.)

GRAND FINALE. San Francisco's Chinatown still holds the record for sponsoring the largest Chinese New Year celebration in the country, drawing hundreds of thousands of people to Chinatown every year. (Photograph by Ben Chan.)

PORTSMOUTH SQUARE TODAY. On any given day, the plaza's benches, tables, and senior center are filled with local residents—chatting, playing Chinese chess, and taking in the air and sunshine. (Courtesy of Chinatown Community Development Center.)

CHINATOWN'S LIVING ROOM. Portsmouth Square continues to serve as a popular gathering place for men and women, the old and the young, and organizations of different religious and political persuasions. (Photograph by Ben Chan.)

BIBLIOGRAPHY

Chen, Yong. *Chinese San Francisco, 1850-1943: A Trans-Pacific Community*. Stanford: Stanford University Press, 2000.

"The Chinese in California, 1850-1925." Washington, D.C.: Library of Congress, 2003. http://memory.loc.gov/ammem/award99/cubhtml.

Chinn, Thomas W. *Bridging the Pacific: San Francisco Chinatown and Its People*. San Francisco: Chinese Historical Society of America, 1989.

Choy, Philip P. "The Architecture of San Francisco Chinatown." *Chinese America: History and Perspectives, 1990:* 37–66.

Dicker, Laverne Mau. *The Chinese in San Francisco: A Pictorial History*. New York: Dover Publications, 1979.

Dobie, Charles Caldwell. *San Francisco's Chinatown*. New York: D. Appleton-Century Company, 1936.

Kao, George. *Cathay by the Bay: Glimpses of San Francisco's Chinatown in the Year 1950*. Hong Kong: The Chinese Press, 1988.

Lee, Anthony W. *Picturing Chinatown: Art and Orientalism in San Francisco*. Berkeley: University of California Press, 2001.

Loo, Chalsa M. *Chinese America: Mental Health and Quality of Life in the Inner City*. Thousand Oaks: Sage Publications, 1998.

Nee, Victor G. and Brett De Bary. *Longtime Californ': A Documentary Study of an American Chinatown*. New York: Pantheon Books, 1972.

Tchen, John Kuo Wei. *Genthe's Photographs of San Francisco's Old Chinatown*. New York: Dover Publications, 1984.

Yip, Christopher Lee. "San Francisco's Chinatown: An Architectural and Urban History." Ph.D. Dissertation, University of California, Berkeley, 1995.

Yung, Judy. *Unbound Feet: A Social History of Chinese Women in San Francisco*. Berkeley: University of California Press, 1995.

Key to Historic Sites in Chinatown

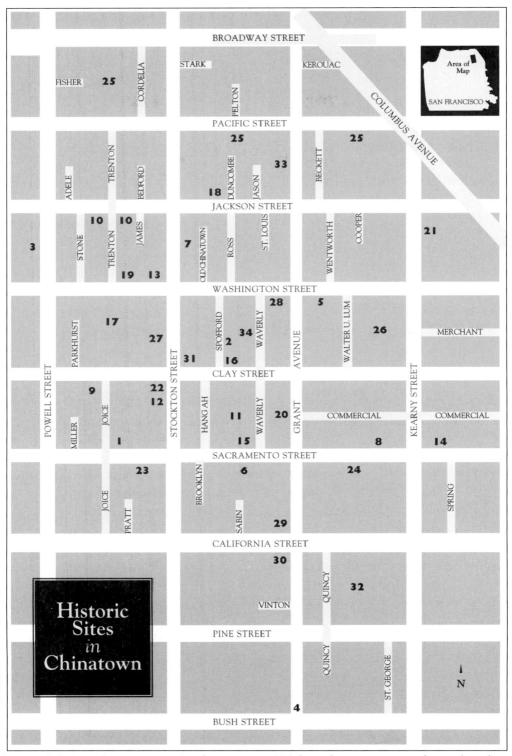

STREET MAP OF CHINATOWN. See key on page 126 for information on each numbered site. (Graphics by Elaine Joe.)

ACROSS AMERICA, PEOPLE ARE DISCOVERING
SOMETHING WONDERFUL. *THEIR HERITAGE.*

Arcadia Publishing is the leading local history publisher in the United States. With more than 3,000 titles in print and hundreds of new titles released every year, Arcadia has extensive specialized experience chronicling the history of communities and celebrating America's hidden stories, bringing to life the people, places, and events from the past. To discover the history of other communities across the nation, please visit:

www.arcadiapublishing.com

Customized search tools allow you to find regional history books about the town where you grew up, the cities where your friends and family live, the town where your parents met, or even that retirement spot you've been dreaming about.